The Halifax Explosion

Surviving the Blast that Shook a Nation

by Joyce Glasner

For my husband, Doug

PUBLISHED BY ALTITUDE PUBLISHING CANADA LTD.
1500 Railway Avenue, Canmore, Alberta T1W 1P6
www.altitudepublishing.com
www.amazingstories.ca
1-800-957-6888

Based on a book with the same title
by Joyce Glasner, first published in 2003.

Publisher	Stephen Hutchings
Associate Publisher	Kara Turner
Junior Edition Series Editor	Linda Aspen-Baxter
Layout	Zoe Howes

We acknowledge the financial support of the Government
of Canada through the Book Publishing Industry Development
Program (BPIDP) for our publishing activities.

Altitude GreenTree Program
Altitude Publishing will plant twice as many trees as were used
in the manufacturing of this product.

Library and Archives Canada Cataloguing in Publication Data

ISBN 10: 1-55439-707-3
ISBN 13: 978-1-55439-707-5

Printed and bound in Canada by Friesens
2 4 6 8 9 7 5 3 1

Contents

A plan of Halifax c. 1910

Prologue

Billy Wells jammed the gas pedal to the floor. He blew the horn. Then he pulled out to pass a team of Clydesdales hauling a wagon. The sound of the horn startled the horses. They whinnied shrilly and broke into a trot.

"Take it easy, Billy!" Chief Cordon shouted. His words were hard to hear. The bells on the fire truck were clanging, and the engine was roaring. "Patricia" was the station's new motorized fire engine. Driving Patricia at top speed through the city thrilled Billy.

Up ahead, a column of black smoke billowed high above the harbour. It looked bad. Billy had never seen anything quite like it. He couldn't imagine the fire that would make that much smoke.

The firefighters arrived at the wharf. They saw a blazing ship butted up against Pier 6. Flames flickered high above the freighter's deck. Fire had spilled from its bow down onto the wharf. The surrounding buildings had burst into flames. The heat from the blaze was intense. The men had to shield their faces as they drew near.

Suddenly, the earth shook violently. Billy was ripped from the driver's seat. He was tossed through the air. The next thing he knew, he was on the ground several metres from the fire engine. Before he had a chance to move, he was swept up in a massive tidal wave. The powerful force of the wave drove him along for several metres. Then it slammed him against a telephone pole.

When the water drained away, Billy lay in a heap at the foot of the pole. Shrapnel began pelting down around him. Greasy black rain fell from the sky.

When it was all over, Billy struggled to his feet. He looked around in disbelief. He was halfway up Fort Needham Hill. The hill was across the street from the wharf where he'd parked. He felt a throbbing pain in his right arm. Billy looked down. Patricia's steering wheel was gripped tightly in his right hand.

Billy staggered back to Pier 6 in a daze. The fire truck was upside down. It was several metres from where it had been parked. The shiny new vehicle was nothing more than a twisted piece of junk. Scattered around the wreck were a few of the lifeless bodies of his fellow firefighters. The rest were nowhere in sight.

Chapter 1
At the Mouth
of the Harbour

A crescent moon hung in the clear night sky. Its silvery light reflected faintly off the black waters of Halifax Harbour. Every five seconds, the light from the lighthouse on McNab's Island beamed across the water. It lit up the bow of the grey freighter anchored just off shore.

12 a.m. December 6, 1917
Captain Aimé Le Medec could not sleep. He paced back and forth on the deck. The captain and his crew had just finished a nerve-wracking five-day journey from New York. Captain Le Medec had spent 22 years at sea. In all that time, he'd never had a more stressful voyage than the one from New York to Halifax. His next journey would be across the Atlantic Ocean. It would be far worse.

At that time, the waters of the Atlantic were filled with German submarines. Crossing was dangerous for the swiftest of vessels. For safety, most ships travelled in convoys. These were escorted by armed naval vessels. Still, German U-boats had sunk hundreds of Allied ships.

Le Medec's vessel was a battered old freighter named the *Mont Blanc*. It was so heavily loaded, it could barely manage seven knots for any distance. Could the French freighter keep up with any convoy at that speed? The chances were not good.

The *Mont Blanc* was a 3,171 tonne freighter. It was owned and operated by a French shipping company. Now, it was under French naval orders. In ordinary times, the worn out, 18-year-old freighter would never be used for such a mission. But these were not ordinary times. World War I was raging in Europe. Every available vessel was put to work for the war effort. It didn't matter how old and broken down it was.

Deadly Cargo

Before they arrived in New York, Le Medec had not been told what they were to transport back to France. He was shocked when he saw what the stevedores were loading onboard. They filled the hold with 2,337 tonnes of picric acid, 203 tonnes of TNT, and 10 tonnes of gun cotton. Added to that, 36 tonnes of benzol were rolled on board. Benzol is a highly flammable liquid. Le Medec had no past experience with explosives. Still, he knew this was enough deadly material to blow the *Mont Blanc* — and anything within range — to smithereens.

Care had been taken to stow the explosive cargo safely in the hold. The drums of benzol were strapped snugly on deck away from the other materials. Still, it was disturbing to think of sailing across the Atlantic on a floating bomb.

Once the vessel was loaded, Le Medec received more bad news. The convoy they were supposed to sail with refused to take them along. The freighter would have to sail up the coast to Halifax on its own. In Halifax, a larger convoy might accept the *Mont Blanc*. However, the *Mont Blanc* was slow. It was also carrying deadly cargo. It was possible that no convoy would accept them. In that case, they would have to try to cross the Atlantic on their own.

Halifax Harbour

The *Mont Blanc* arrived at Halifax Harbour late in the afternoon. They were told to dock in the examination anchorage. This was just off McNab's Island. There, they met Frances Mackey, the harbour pilot. Mackey would guide the freighter into the harbour. When he came aboard, the pilot had more bad news for Le Medec. A string of mines was stretched across the harbour entrance every evening. This was known as the anti-submarine net. It kept enemy vessels from entering the harbour. Mackey told Le Medec the net was already in place. The *Mont Blanc* would have to spend the night anchored off McNab's Island. Le Medec was anxious to get into the harbour. He asked Mackey to stay aboard that night. That way, they could get started as soon as the boom opened at dawn.

Halifax Harbour was an ideal Allied naval port during the war. The city of Halifax sits on a large peninsula that juts out into the harbour. This peninsula narrows the channel between Dartmouth and Halifax. The south end of the peninsula overlooks McNab's Island. Beyond that lie the open waters of the Atlantic Ocean. The north end of the peninsula faces Bedford Basin, an almost completely enclosed body of water. This arrangement meant the harbour was easy to secure. By 1917, the harbour was bustling with Allied cruisers, freighters, and merchant ships. Bedford Basin was often crowded with vessels awaiting convoy.

In times of peace, Halifax was a small, quiet city. It had a population of about 50,000. However, the population grew quickly once the war began. Citadel Hill was the dividing line between the city's north and south ends. The upper classes lived in the South End. This area was known for its elegant tree-lined avenues and Victorian mansions.

North End Halifax was home to the working class. The North End was heavily industrialized. Factories were scattered throughout. Richmond was the heart of the city's North End. It sat on the steep eastern slope of Fort Needham. Richmond's dirt streets were lined with simple, wood framed houses. These were the homes of the men and women who worked in the area's dockyards and factories.

To Captain Aimé Le Medec, Halifax was just another port city. It was nothing more than a safe haven in dangerous times. That night, the city was almost invisible from where he stood. All he could see were a few faint lights twinkling off in the distance.

Chapter 2
Port City Morning

A t 7:30 a.m., Vincent Coleman stepped outside and took a deep breath. It was a bright, sunny morning. The weather had been very mild for that time of year. The ground was still bare, and the air was pleasantly crisp. A whiff of briny ocean scent drifted up from the harbour. A light mist hung over the glassy water. Along Barrington Street, workers were making their way to the factories and dockyards along the waterfront.

That December morning, Vincent Coleman had every reason to feel good about his life. Things finally seemed to be falling into place for him. His job as a train dispatcher with the Canadian Government Railway was going well. True, he was barely making enough to support his family. However, the union had promised there would soon be raises for everyone. Vincent, his wife Frances, and their four children — Nita, Gerald, Eleanor, and Aileen (nicknamed "Babe") — had just moved into their first new home. It was a large two-storey house on the corner of Russell and Albert. It had taken years of scrimping to save enough to buy their own home. A pay raise would make life easier for the family.

The past few years had been hard for the Colemans. Their two sons, Gerald and Cyril, had caught diphtheria the year before. Diphtheria is a life-threatening disease. It spreads easily from person to person. The boys were kept away from the other children. During their illness, Frances nursed them day and night.

Gerald was the older of the two boys. He survived the deadly disease. However, his eight-year-old brother Cyril did not. The couple was heartbroken over the loss of their youngest son. However, Frances was a strong woman. Her strength held the family together during that difficult time.

Moving into the new house seemed like a fresh start for the Colemans. It was a chance to leave the bad times behind.

After their father left for work that morning, the children sat down to breakfast. While they ate, Frances got their clothes ready. Nita was the Colemans' oldest daughter. She had just come down with strep throat, so she was staying home that day. Her brother Gerald didn't have classes until that afternoon. However, he had to go to St. Joseph's Church. He was serving as an altar boy at morning mass. That meant Eleanor was the only one going to school that morning.

Across town, Jean Forrest and her parents had just finished breakfast. As they rose from the table there was a knock at the door. It was the plumbers Mr. Forrest had hired to fix some leaking pipes. Jean was annoyed that the men had arrived so early. She had a busy day ahead at the Red Cross Hospital. The plumbers would be in her way as she tried to get ready for work.

North Street Station was bustling that morning. Sailors and soldiers crowded the big stone building. People from the outskirts of the city hurried through the station on their way to work. All the hustle and bustle seemed very exciting to 15-year-old Evelyn Fox. Her family had just moved to Bedford from a small community on the coast. Bedford was a suburb of Halifax. Most mornings, Evelyn travelled in from Bedford aboard the 8:20 train. That morning, she was up earlier than usual. She decided to travel with her father on the train that left at 7:30 a.m. The trip into the city was uneventful. Evelyn used the half-hour to finish her homework.

Evelyn attended the Halifax County Academy. It was a large brick building at the foot of Citadel Hill on Brunswick Street. Her father was principal of Alexandra School. After leaving the station, father and daughter walked up North Street to Brunswick. There, they said goodbye and went their separate ways.

Dean John Llwyd was up early that morning. He always tried to spend some time on his writing before his official duties began. Llwyd had moved to Halifax five years earlier. At that time, he became Rector of All Saints Cathedral. Since then, he had become the Dean of Nova Scotia. Llwyd wasn't a full-time writer, but he had had several poems, articles, and essays published. His writing was important to him, but his family and ministerial duties came first. That left little time to spend on his writing. Therefore, these quiet early morning hours were precious.

The day had started like most others. No one in the city could have imagined it would soon become a nightmare.

Chapter 3
A Fateful Error

The first officer and Francis Mackey stood beside Captain Le Medec on the bridge. They watched an American freighter steam into the harbour ahead of them. At last, they were given the signal to enter. As they crept towards the outer boom, Le Medec breathed a sigh of relief.

Mackey spoke no French and Le Medec knew little English. Still, they managed to communicate. Mackey had been guiding vessels in and out of Halifax Harbour for 25 years. He knew the harbour as well as his own backyard. Every inlet, shoal, and shallow were etched in his memory. This was Le Medec's first trip to Halifax. He was thankful that the pilot knew the harbour so well.

Visibility was good that morning. It looked like it would be smooth sailing into the harbour. Before long, they passed through the outer boom. Le Medec began to relax for the first time since leaving New York. If all went well, they would soon be joining a convoy. Then they'd be on their way back to France. As far as Le Medec was concerned, the sooner this voyage was over the better.

Traffic in the harbour was heavy that morning. Every pier swarmed with stevedores. The men were busy loading and unloading shipments of lumber, food, and horses. In Bedford Basin, cruisers and merchant ships awaited convoy. In the Narrows, freighters lined up for berths.

A Close Call

At 8:15, Captain Horatio Brannen and his crew set out from the dry docks. They were towing two scows of ashes. Brannen's vessel was the tug *SS Stella Maris*. At that time, it was chartered by the Royal Canadian Navy (RCN). That morning, Brannen's orders were to haul the ashes into the Bedford Basin. This was a routine job for Brannen and his crew. The skipper didn't foresee any problems. Just as they started crossing the harbour, a ship came steaming through the Narrows. The vessel was heading straight towards them. Brannen had two awkward scows in tow. They'd never make it across the harbour in time to avoid a collision. He decided to swing his vessel back to the Halifax side. He made it back to shore just as the steamer sailed by. He noted the name

Imo on the bow. The words "BELGIAN RELIEF" were written in bold, red letters on its hull.

The *Imo* was a 5,122 tonne Norwegian tramp steamer. It was taking supplies from North America to the war-torn nation of Belgium. The *Imo* should have been halfway down the eastern seaboard by that time. Instead, it had spent the day before waiting for a coal shipment. The shipment had arrived late. By the time the coal was loaded, the anti-submarine net was in place. That meant they had to spend an extra night in port.

Captain Hakkom From was furious about the delay. He was anxious to proceed to New York. There, they were to pick up a load of grain. Captain From wanted to make up time. He wanted pilot William Hays to speed up their passage through the harbour. Hays did what he was asked. He pushed the steamer a full two knots over the harbour's speed limit of five knots.

The *Imo* sped through the Narrows. As it did, it met the American freighter that had sailed through the boom ahead of the *Mont Blanc*. The freighter was heading into the Bedford Basin. However, it was too far into the *Imo*'s water to correct its course. Ships usually pass each other port-to-port. (Port is the left hand side of the ship when it is facing forwards.) Rather than do that, the skipper of the American ship signalled that he was maintaining course to the left. This meant the two vessels would pass starboard to starboard. (Starboard is the right hand side of the ship when it is facing forwards.) The *Imo* signalled that it understood. The two ships steamed by one another without difficulty. After passing the American freighter, the *Imo* stayed on the same course.

The Collision

Captain Brannen, his first mate (and son), Walter Brannen, and William Knickerson stood on the bridge of the *Stella Maris* . They kept a close watch on the *Imo* as it barrelled through the busy harbour. All three had a bad feeling about the ship's pace. Suddenly, the *Mont Blanc* appeared. It was heading towards them from the opposite direction. Brannen could see something was wrong. The *Imo* was too far into what should have been the French ship's path.

The *Mont Blanc* gave one short whistle blast to signal it was changing course to starboard. The *Imo* responded with two blasts. This signalled that it was going to change its course to port. This shift would put the *Imo* even deeper into the French freighter's water. The two ships tried to move around one another. As they did, a flurry of whistle blasts rang out across the harbour. The *Imo* was bearing down fast on the French freighter. Something was terribly wrong. Unless a miracle occurred, the two ships would collide. Just then, the *Mont Blanc's* bow swung hard to port.

"They're going to collide!" William Knickerson shouted.

Captain Brannen could not believe what he was

seeing. The *Imo* moved steadily towards the French ship. The gap closed between the two ships. Then suddenly, the *Imo*'s bow slammed into the *Mont Blanc*'s starboard bow.

Captain Aimé Le Medec watched in horror as the Norwegian ship's bow cut a three-metre gash in his starboard bow. He was stunned by the accident, but he quickly pulled himself together. He ordered the engines reversed. Captain From did the same. As the *Imo*'s bow withdrew from the gash, the grinding of metal on metal filled the air. The friction created a spray of sparks. The sparks showered across the deck of the French freighter.

Several of the drums of benzol had broken free from their lashings. They began to leak. It wasn't long before the sparks hit the benzol. In a matter of minutes, the *Mont Blanc*'s deck was in flames. Clouds of black smoke billowed high above the deck. One by one, the drums of benzol began to explode. Each one added more fuel to the fire.

The situation was grim. Le Medec struggled to stay calm. He tried to think of a way to fight the blaze. He could see the crew were beginning to panic. They were well aware of the danger they were in. Throughout the journey, they had not been able to smoke or carry matches because of the fire hazard. They knew if the flames reached the TNT in the hold, the vessel would explode.

Abandon Ship!

Le Medec's only real option was to try to sink the ship before it blew. The question was, did he have time? The bolts on the hatches were badly rusted. It would take time to loosen the bolts, open the valves, and flood the compartments. By then, the powder keg they were standing on would surely explode. All aboard would be killed.

Le Medec decided there was only one thing he could do. He had to try to save his crew. He gave the order to abandon ship.

By that time, the men had already lowered the two lifeboats into the water. As soon as the order was given, they scurried down ladders and ropes. They wanted to get as far from the vessel as they could. The first officer made sure all hands were in the lifeboats. Then he reported to the captain. He told Le Medec that the men were waiting for him to join them. However, Le Medec did not plan to abandon ship. He believed it was a captain's duty to go down with his vessel. He told the first officer that he was staying aboard. He held his ground. The first officer realized that there was no time to argue the point. He grabbed his captain and forced him down the ladder into the waiting lifeboat.

Chapter 4
The Red Flag

All activity onshore stopped at the sight of the burning ship in the harbour. Dockworkers dropped what they were doing. They gathered in groups along the wharves to watch the action. Factory workers, schoolchildren, and housewives rushed to windows. They watched in awe as the *Mont Blanc* drifted steadily towards Pier 6.

Meanwhile, Charles Duggan Jr. hurried down to the dock. Like his father, Charles was a ferry pilot. He had grown up on the harbour. He felt more at home on water than on land. Like most seafarers, Charles was ready to risk his own safety to help save others. He had seen the collision of the two ships. Now he was on his way to offer help. He hopped aboard his launch and started the engine.

Charles cleared the wharf and set off towards the *Mont Blanc*. As he neared the vessel, he saw the crew of the burning ship. They were spilling over the side "like rats." Once they were in the boats, they rowed away as fast as they could. Charles was worried that there might still be crew aboard. He kept moving towards the ship. He got close enough to "feel the heat of the fire" on his face. Then he cut the engine.

Meanwhile, Fred Longland was reporting for duty on HMCS *Niobe*. Longland had just arrived in Halifax that morning. He was an officer with the Royal Canadian Navy.

Since it was no longer seaworthy, the *Niobe* was moored at the dockyards. There, it served as a training and depot vessel. Fred Longland reported to the drafting officer onboard. Then he made his way up top. The movements of the *Mont Blanc* and *Imo* caught his eye. He paused to watch. The frantic exchange of whistle blasts were signs of trouble. Longland realized the two ships were on a collision course. Within minutes, the ships collided. Fred rushed to the forecastle deck to get a better view.

Word quickly spread that a ship was on fire in the harbour. The *Niobe* was sending a crew in the steam pinnace to help fight the fire. Soon, the forecastle deck was packed with curious sailors. They were all trying to get a good view of the action.

Heroic Actions

Meanwhile, Captain Brannen had ordered his crew to turn the *Stella Maris* back to the dry dock. He planned to drop off the scows. Then they would head towards the burning ship to offer help. Captain Horatio Brannen had been in the salvage business for nearly 20 years. He had conducted many daring rescue operations over the years. He was well known and widely respected for these rescues. This fire looked worse than any he'd seen.

Before long, the tug approached the burning freighter. Brannen ordered his first mate to break out the hose and prepare to fight the blaze.

At the same time, Captain Garnett watched the action from the bridge of the British cruiser, HMS *Highflyer*. Captain Garnett didn't know about the deadly cargo in the *Mont Blanc's* hold. Nonetheless, he was concerned. A burning ship so close to others was a hazard. It didn't matter what it was carrying. Many ships nearby had munitions on board. Fire and explosives were a lethal mix.

Captain Garnett decided something had to be done about the fire. He summoned his first officer, Commander Tom Triggs, to the bridge. Garnett ordered Triggs to send an officer over to the burning freighter. He was to assess the situation. Triggs volunteered to go himself. Within minutes, Commander Triggs and a crew of six set off in *Highflyer's* whaler.

By this time, a crowd had gathered outside Uphams

General Store on Barrington Street. Uphams overlooked the Narrows. It offered a perfect view. The store owner noticed that the burning ship was drifting dangerously close to Pier 6. He rushed inside to call the fire department. Before long, the fire engines were on their way. The clanging of bells echoed across the city as the trucks raced to the scene.

The Terrible Secret

Few people knew what the *Mont Blanc* carried in its hold. The nature of the cargo had been kept secret on purpose. Normally when a vessel had explosives on board, it flew a red flag. This warned others of the harmful nature of the cargo. However, the *Mont Blanc* had not hoisted the red flag before it entered the harbour. It was widely believed that enemy spies were in the area. To be safe, Le Medec had decided not to fly the red flag. As a result, few in the city were aware that the burning ship was a great threat.

Commander James Murray was one of the few who knew about the explosives. He was the Transport Officer Liaison between the Port Convoy Office and the merchant ships. When the collision occurred, Murray was returning from the Bedford Basin. As soon as his tug entered the Narrows, the commander saw the burning vessel. He quickly swung the tug into Pier 9. Would he be able to reach his office and send out a general alarm before it was too late?

The minute the tug docked, he leaped to the wharf. On the way to his office, he ran into a sailor. Murray ordered the sailor to warn everyone in the area that the burning ship was loaded with munitions. It could blow up at any moment.

The *Mont Blanc* was now very close to Pier 6. The railway yardmaster's building sat a little less than 200 metres away from the pier. Inside were dispatcher Vincent Coleman and chief clerk William Lovette. They watched anxiously. Coleman and Lovette knew the fire posed a serious threat to the yardmaster's building. It was also a danger to the dozens of freight cars standing in the yards. Suddenly, the ship slammed into the jetty. Within minutes, fire spilled from the deck onto the pier. It ignited the wooden pilings and nearby sheds.

By then, the *Stella Maris* was alongside the blazing *Mont Blanc.* Captain Brannen and his crew were bravely trying to put out the raging inferno. Commander Triggs and his crew from the *Highflyer* arrived on the scene. Triggs could see that trying to fight the blaze with one hose was hopeless. He boarded the *Stella Maris* to talk with Brannen. They decided to attach a line to the *Mont Blanc.* Then they would tow it away from the pier. Out in mid-channel, it would pose less of a threat. This would also allow other tugs to get close enough to help fight the fire. While Brannen and Triggs discussed the plan, *Niobe's* steam pinnace arrived on the scene.

Triggs was certain that Captain Brannen could

handle the situation. He left the scene and set out towards the *Imo*. He wanted to assess its damage. After the collision, the Norwegian steamer had drifted into mid-channel. There, it remained.

Meanwhile, Francis Mackey and the crew of the *Mont Blanc* were rowing furiously towards the Dartmouth shore. At the small settlement of Tuft's Cove, a group had gathered on the beach. They were watching the burning ship. The French sailors got to shore and clambered out of the lifeboats. They tried to warn the people on the beach to run for cover. The sailors shouted and pointed at the burning ship and then at the woods. However, the spectators didn't understand French. They just stared curiously at the sailors. Finally, one sailor came up with a plan to get the people away from the shore. He snatched a baby from a woman's arms and sprinted off into the woods. The mother, and everyone nearby, followed close on his heels.

In the harbour, Charles Duggan sat a short distance from the blazing *Mont Blanc*. He saw the *Stella Maris* and the whaler from the *Highflyer* pull alongside. He figured the navy had everything under control. They probably wouldn't need his help. He started up the launch. He was just swinging around to head back to shore when he heard a series of explosions. He turned to see the barrels of benzol on the *Mont Blanc's* deck lifting in the air. They burst into flames "with a roar." Charles knew he was in danger. He opened up the throttle and sped towards the Dartmouth shore.

Meanwhile, Vincent Coleman and William Lovette were still in the railway yardmaster's office. They were debating. Should they clear out or not?

The sailor sent by Commander Murray suddenly appeared at the door. "That ship's loaded with explosives and about to blow!" he shouted. Then he disappeared.

The two men didn't think twice. They rushed out the door and across the tracks towards Barrington Street. After a few seconds, William sensed that the dispatcher was no longer behind him. He turned to see his friend running back towards the office. He hollered at Vincent. What was he doing? The dispatcher just kept running. He shouted over his shoulder something about the Number 10 Train being due in at any minute. He had to warn Rockingham to hold it up.

Chapter 5
Shock Waves

At 9:06 a.m., 3,171 tonnes of iron and steel exploded into millions of fragments. They flew for kilometres in all directions. The blast ripped through the city. Its force and fury was beyond imagination. In the blink of an eye, the community of Richmond was flattened. Halifax and Dartmouth were devastated. Houses collapsed, factories toppled, and churches crumbled. Ships, trains, and automobiles were hurled about like children's toys. Roads were wiped out. Railway tracks were torn from the earth. Trees and telephone poles snapped like matchsticks. Debris scattered everywhere. The blast shattered every window for many kilometres. Shards of glass ripped through flesh and lodged in people's eyeballs. Gas lines ruptured. Live coals from hundreds of stoves spilled out onto the heaps of kindling created by the blast.

An oily black substance rained down from above. Shrapnel battered the ruins for several minutes.

The harbour became a seething cauldron. Its floor split open and hurled boulders up from the deep. The force of the blast created a tidal wave. The wave swamped the shore. Small ships were swallowed and spit back out. Large vessels were ripped from their moorings and flung to shore.

When it was all over, at least 1,900 people were dead and 9,000 were injured. Hundreds were blinded for life. Thousands of people were left homeless. In addition, electricity, gas, telephone, and telegraph lines were all cut. Halifax was completely crippled.

In the Harbour

Charles Duggan was halfway across the harbour when he looked back. He would never forget the sight. The blazing ship "seemed to settle in the water. A lurid yellowish-green spurt of flame rose towards the heavens and drove ahead of it a cloud of smoke, which must have risen 200 feet (61 m) in the air." Then came the loudest crash he had ever heard. His launch seemed to be snatched from beneath his feet. He was plunged into the icy harbour. He was "engulfed in a swirling, roaring mass of water." It drove him to the bottom "like a stone." After what seemed like an eternity, he surfaced. Then he was caught up in a second raging wave. This time, he was knocked unconscious.

The situation in the harbour was desperate. A cloud of thick, black smoke hung over the water. Ravaged ships drifted helplessly on the currents. Bodies and debris littered the surface. The *Stella Maris* was closest to the *Mont Blanc* when it exploded. The tug had taken the full force of the blast. Amazingly, the vessel was not totally demolished. Instead, it was blown downstream. It came to rest near the dry dock. It was stripped of its smokestack and spars. However, it was still intact. Captain Horatio Brannen and 18 of his crew were killed instantly. Luckily, William Knickerson and Walter Brannen were driven below deck by the blast. They were injured, but both men survived.

Highflyer's whaler was also hit hard by the explosion. Lieutenant Commander Tom Triggs was killed instantly. A few of his crew survived. The *Imo* was hurled onto the Dartmouth shore. Its superstructure was demolished. Captain Hakkom From and pilot William Hayes were both killed in the blast.

The *Niobe* was also badly battered. A hail of "boiler tubes, rivets, and jagged steel plates" from the *Mont Blanc* had hammered the deck. The crew had scrambled for cover to escape from the storm of flying debris. Men had stuffed themselves into ventilator shafts, down stairwells, and beneath lifeboats.

Then the tidal wave hit. The wave ripped the massive vessel from its moorings. It was heaved high into the air. Then it was slammed back to the surface. When it was all over, *Niobe*'s main deck was a mess. All four of the ship's funnels were demolished. Its superstructure was destroyed. In all, 19 men were dead. Dozens were severely wounded.

There had been 45 vessels in Halifax Harbour that morning. Almost every one was seriously damaged. In addition, the dockyards, Naval College, and several wharves were in ruins. For the first time in its history, Halifax Harbour was completely paralyzed.

Terror and Turmoil

In Richmond, the students were saying morning prayers at St. Joseph's School when the blast occurred. Seven-year-old Eleanor Coleman felt the building tremble. This was followed by a huge crash. A nun had been leading the prayers. She screamed something about the Germans attacking. The ceiling began to sag and crack. Chunks of plaster began falling on the frightened girls. Eleanor's first thoughts were of her mother and her sisters, Babe and Nita. They were just down the street. If the Germans *were* attacking, what would happen to them?

The nun got the girls out of the room just minutes before the ceiling came crashing down. The girls picked their way through the rubble in the hallways. Every now and then, they heard sobbing and cries for help coming from the other rooms.

St. Joseph's was a total wreck. The explosion had

The battered *Imo*

ripped off most of the roof. The floors had collapsed. The students in the Grade 8 classroom were trapped between floors near the top of the building. The stairs had been wiped out. To escape, the children had to climb out the windows. Then they had to jump to the ground.

One of the nuns had been blinded when flying glass struck her in the eyes. In spite of her injury, she knew she had to get the children to safety. She led the girls out of the wreckage by feeling her way along. It was a miracle that only two girls were killed. However, many were seriously injured, including several nuns.

Once outside, Eleanor looked around for her brother Gerald. He had been serving in the morning mass at St. Joseph's Church next door. Normally, he would have waited for her outside the school. She didn't see him anywhere in the schoolyard so she started to make her way home alone.

As she walked down her street, Eleanor couldn't believe her eyes. Most of the houses along the street were nothing but flaming piles of debris. Everywhere she looked, there were badly wounded people. Many were screaming for help. Smoke stung her eyes and burned her throat. She could barely make her way through the wreckage blocking the street. Eleanor saw one of their neighbours along the street. He was an old man with a wooden leg. His wooden leg was missing. It was sad to see him dragging himself through the ruins of his home.

At last, Eleanor reached the spot where her house should have been. She began to panic. The house was gone. In its place was a smouldering heap of rubble. Nita and Gerald were digging through the piles of splintered boards and plaster. They could hear Babe crying somewhere in the wreckage. The baby's cries made them dig faster. The heat and smoke from the surrounding fires was becoming too much. Still, the children continued to heave boards. They lifted heavy sections of lathe and plaster walls. Finally, they found their mother on the kitchen floor. She was unconscious. Babe was beneath the kitchen sink, a few feet away from her mother. Babe looked unharmed, but their mother was in bad shape.

The fire was drawing closer. The children knew they had to get out of the area fast. Eleanor grabbed the baby. Nita and Gerald carefully lifted their mother from the wreckage. They decided to go back uphill towards the church. They were certain they would find help there. By then, Russell Street was an inferno. The children struggled through the wall of flames. Slowly, they made their way up the steep slope to Gottingen Street.

It was 9:30 a.m. before Frances Coleman regained consciousness. She was lying on the sidewalk on Gottingen Street. She tried to move. A stab of pain shot through her back. Nita and Gerald were hovering over her. Their soot-smeared faces were filled with worry.

Where was Babe? Was she all right?

Nita told her mother that the baby was fine. Eleanor was looking after her. Frances was relieved by this news, but she was puzzled. The last thing she remembered was having coffee with her sister-in-law in the kitchen. Then there was a "terrible crack."

Her sister-in-law had jumped up and cried, "Oh my God, the Germans are here!"

What on earth had happened? Why was she lying out on the cold sidewalk? Gerald explained that a ship had blown up in the harbour. The explosion had flattened everything for kilometres. Suddenly,

Frances thought of her husband, Vincent. Was he okay? Another stab of pain shot through her. Again, everything went black.

City under Seige

Jean Forrest was getting ready for work when the explosion occurred. Her first thought was that a German fleet had slipped through the harbour's defences. She was certain the city was under siege. Jean and her parents scrambled for the safety of the cellar. The plumbers who were working in the house followed close behind.

Jean had been prepared for something like this. She followed the war news closely. German U-boats had been getting closer and closer to North America over the past few months. She believed the war would land on these shores in time.

There was a period of quiet. Jean decided there was no point staying in the cellar any longer. Her parents begged her not to leave. Jean had to go. She had to know what had caused the blast. She left the others and went out into the streets. The first thing she saw was the cloud of smoke over the North End of the city. She figured the magazine must have blown up. If so, she would be needed at the Red Cross headquarters. Jean hurried off in that direction.

At the Halifax County Academy, the students had just finished singing the morning hymn. Suddenly, the brick building "rocked and shook." A "tremendous booming roar" was heard. Plaster and glass rained down on them. Evelyn Fox held onto the chair in front of her until the torrent died down. She thought the Germans must have been shelling the school.

Almost everyone in the city shared the same thought that morning. This wasn't too surprising. Only the week before frightening headlines had appeared in a local paper. They had alarmed people about the possibility of such an attack. Now, it seemed that assault had finally begun.

For several seconds after the blast, all the students sat perfectly still. They waited anxiously for another strike. Nothing happened. The principal led everyone down the fire escape to the schoolyard. There, Evelyn was struck by the complete silence of the city. It seemed to be holding its breath. She had expected soldiers to be swarming the streets. It was too quiet. It wasn't natural. The quiet chilled Evelyn more than the cool morning air. Someone pointed to the plume of smoke in the sky over the North End. To Evelyn, it looked like "a grey mushroom on a thick pallid stalk." She would never forget that sight.

While the morning hymn was being sung at the Halifax Academy, Dean John Llwyd was at All Saint's Cathedral. He was leading morning prayers. He felt the earth tremble beneath his feet. "A German shell!" he thought. He paused and looked up at the congregation. There were only three worshippers in the

Many buildings were totally flattened

chapel that morning. They were his wife, Marie, and two other women. A few seconds passed in complete silence. Llwyd cleared his throat. Then he picked up where he'd left off. Suddenly, an earth-shattering roar drowned out his words. The stone building shuddered. Large windows lined the north side of the building. Each of them shattered. A blizzard of glass showered down on the pews. The women gasped and shrieked. Llwyd felt his knees go weak. Was the building going to tumble down on them? In all his 56 years, he had never been so frightened.

Finally, the terrifying moment passed. Dean Llwyd ran to the doorway. The solid oak doors were ripped from their hinges. He looked out to see a cloud of yellowish-grey smoke rising high in the sky. It curled and billowed higher and higher. Llwyd returned to his congregation.

"It's all over. It must have been a munitions explosion at some point north," he said. "We can go on and finish our service."

The women were clearly shaken by what had happened. Marie's hat had been blown off her head. It lay on the floor near the altar. Llwyd decided to cut the service short. He said a few more prayers. Then he led the women outside.

Llwyd took Marie home. Then he headed downtown to find out what had happened. He was sure that there would be wounded needing his help. At Spring Garden Road, Llwyd ran into a member of his congregation. Mr. Hewat had just come in on the train from Truro. He told Llwyd that the explosion had lifted the train from the tracks. Hewat and the other passengers had been forced to get off before Richmond. They had walked through the devastated area. Hewat tried to describe the tragic sights he'd seen in the North End. As he did, his voice shook.

"Everywhere houses razed to the ground; buildings of considerable size, mere heaps of bricks," he said. "Fire has started, and the wounded and dying are lying around in twos and threes."

Llwyd was amazed by Hewat's story. He was anxious to get to the disaster area. Llwyd flagged down a passing vehicle. He asked the driver to take him to the North Street Station. The station stood on the edge of the devastated area. It was a large stone building. A glass canopy had covered the platforms and tracks. Now, the building looked as though it had been bombarded. The glass roof had come crashing down on the tracks. Splintered timbers and debris covered the battered cars. Glass lay in glittering drifts everywhere.

Wellington Barracks

Wellington Barracks was a large military compound. It was located just above the dockyards on Barrington Street. The compound housed the men's quarters, officers' quarters, married quarters, and the magazine. This was a small building where munitions were stored.

At the time, the barracks was home to the 76th Regiment. Its main purpose was local guard duty. That morning, the band played as the men marched into the parade square. Then they lined up for inspection.

Lieutenant Charles MacLennan and three friends stood at the north end of the compound. They had a good view of the fire in the harbour. They had never seen such a spectacular fire. The three discussed what might have caused the flames to shoot to the top of the tall column of black smoke.

"Oil barrels vaporizing," MacLennan suggested.

The next thing he knew, he was face down on the ground. He quickly jumped up and leaped into a nearby moat for cover. For several minutes, MacLennan lay there with his head down. Shrapnel hammered the ground around him. The barrage finally let up. MacLennan climbed out of the moat. He was unhurt, but a bit shaken.

The garrison was in a state of chaos. Only minutes before, rows of perfectly groomed soldiers had stood at attention in the parade square. Now it was strewn with wounded men, broken rifles, backpacks, and chunks of debris. One of those wounded was the orderly officer. His thigh had been shattered by a piece of shrapnel.

For the moment, the battalion had no leader.

Chapter 6
Beyond the Call of Duty

The first thing Henry Colwell noticed when he arrived at City Hall that morning was the clock tower. The hands of the clock were frozen at 9:06. Colwell was Halifax's deputy mayor. The mayor happened to be out of town that day. That meant Colwell had to take the lead in dealing with the crisis. He faced every leader's worst nightmare. All communication with the outside world had been cut. The city's emergency services had completely broken down. Half of the city was on fire, and the fire department was in chaos. The fire chief and several firefighters had been killed. To make matters worse, its only motorized vehicle had been destroyed. The city police force was in a little better shape, but it was not equipped to deal with a disaster like this. The city's hospitals were also in turmoil. There were hordes of badly injured people. They flooded into every medical facility and doctor's office in Halifax and Dartmouth. In addition, thousands of citizens were suddenly homeless. They were in need of food, shelter, clothing, and most of all, medical care. The situation was dire.

If anyone could deal with such a disaster, it was Henry Colwell. He was a born leader. Colwell quickly took stock of the situation and got to work. Rescuing those trapped in the ruins was the top priority. Next was relief. In order to provide rescue and relief, he needed a lot of manpower. In Halifax at that time, the military was the only organization he could turn to. They had the skills and manpower to contain the damage, help put out the fires, and rescue the injured. Since the phones were out, Colwell and the city clerk walked over to Colonel W. E. Thompson's office. There, they put in an official request for military aid.

Before long, the military had swung into action. Rescue parties were formed. Then the disaster area was roped off. Only rescue workers were allowed in. They began combing the area for victims trapped in the ruins. Any they found were transported to hospitals. Meanwhile, others were busy setting up a tent city on the Commons. It would provide temporary shelter for some of the homeless.

In the days following the explosion, soldiers performed above and beyond the call of duty. They worked around the clock. They often risked their own lives to rescue others. They passed out blankets and food to the victims. They gave up their beds. Many even gave the coats off their backs to those in greater need.

A few hours after the explosion, the Canadian Government Railway got word of the disaster. It responded right away. Relief trains were organized to transport doctors, nurses, and medical supplies to the city. Within hours, aid began pouring in from all parts of Atlantic Canada and the Eastern United States.

On the Dartmouth Shore

Charles Duggan came to onshore. He had no idea how long he had been unconscious. Nor did he know where he was or how he had gotten there. The last thing he remembered was watching the huge cloud of smoke rising from the burning ship. He sat up and looked around. Finally, he realized he was on the Dartmouth shore, near the French Cable Wharf. In fact, he was almost directly across the harbour from his parents' home. Up ahead, Charles saw what looked like the remains of his boat. It had been flung ashore. Another larger vessel was grounded a little farther down. It was tipped at an odd angle and looked badly damaged.

Charles felt sick and dizzy as he struggled to his feet. He could not believe what he saw. It was a scene from a nightmare. Blackened corpses were scattered along the beach. A thick layer of smoke hung over the water. Here and there, black plumes spiralled upwards. Dozens of smashed ships had been ripped from their moorings. They drifted in the layer of debris floating on the water's surface. The landscape onshore was a charred wilderness. In the distance, Charles heard screams and cries for help.

Charles began to stagger down the shore. His only thought was to get home to his family. He was soaking wet and very cold. Before long, he came upon a general store. He hoped he could get warmed up inside. As soon as he stepped inside, he lost consciousness again. When he came to some time later, he was choking. The store was on fire! Charles couldn't see a thing through the dense smoke. He crawled from the burning building and kept walking towards home.

Somehow, Charles made it to the South Ferry Landing. The ferries were still operating. He boarded the first ferry that docked. During the crossing, he overheard the other passengers. Everyone was talking about the explosion and how the North End of the city was destroyed. Charles thought of his wife Rita and their baby. When he had left the house that morning, Rita and his parents were gathered around the front window. They had been watching the fire onboard the *Mont Blanc*. Charles prayed that the stories he'd overheard about Richmond weren't true.

At Tuft's Cove, Captain Aimé Le Medec pulled himself to his feet. It was a miracle that he was still alive.

Le Medec pulled a pack of cigarettes from his pocket. His hands trembled as he jammed one into his mouth. He groped around in his pockets for a match. Then he remembered. Matches had been banned aboard ship.

The first officer was busy trying to round up the crew for a roll call. Several of the frightened men had run off into the woods. The first officer checked on all the men he could find. Then he made his report to the captain. Amazingly, only one man was seriously injured and needed medical attention. The rest had survived the explosion without a scratch.

Chapter 7
Panic in the Streets

The orderly officer at Wellington Barracks was badly hurt. Lieutenant Charles MacLennan had to take charge of the regiment. MacLennan ordered all those who were able to fall in. Of 100 men, only 15 were not wounded. The troop did a quick tour of the garrison. They checked for fires and took stock of the damage. The brick walls of the two-storey buildings were still standing. They had been strong enough to withstand the explosion. However, all was in ruins inside the buildings. The roofs were smashed in. The windows were shattered. The walls looked as though they'd been hit with a wrecking ball. To make matters worse, stoves had been knocked over. Fires blazed throughout the complex.

The garrison's magazine was also badly damaged.

All the garrison's munitions were stored in the magazine. It was a small building surrounded by an iron fence. It sat in the corner of the compound closest to the harbour. A two-metre chunk of steel plating off the *Mont Blanc* had landed on the iron picket fence. It had left a gaping hole in the fence. The hole was large enough for a man to squeeze through. The building was also in bad shape. The door of the magazine was blown in, and the roof was half gone. Lieutenant MacLennan went inside to check the damage.

It was as black as midnight in the little building. MacLennan couldn't see a thing, but he knew better than to light a match. He groped around in the darkness trying to find out how bad the damage was. The floor of the magazine was lined with wooden gratings. The gratings had been smashed into "kindling wood." The lieutenant thought it felt too hot inside. Fearing the worst, he rushed out to get help.

Fire in the Magazine

MacLennan managed to round up about 20 men. He set them to work clearing the debris out of the magazine. Their orders were to get everything out that could burn. Once the men were working, MacLennan went to check on the furnace room next door. His discovery in that room would trigger a wave of panic throughout the city.

The furnace room had been badly shaken in the

explosion. Coals had spilled out of the furnace onto the floor. They had ignited. Now, flames licked the walls close to an open duct. That duct led right to the munitions storage area. If the flames reached the munitions, a second explosion would rock the city. MacLennan had no time to waste. He grabbed a nearby fire extinguisher. He began fighting the flames.

In time, Lieutenant MacLennan was able to douse the fire. However, smoke and steam billowed out through the hole in the roof and the open door. It could be seen by everyone in the area. The men working in the magazine noticed the smoke first. They thought the building was on fire. That meant the munitions would be about to explode. They ran for their lives.

A group of civilians stood outside the garrison fence. When they saw soldiers and sailors fleeing from the burning building, they were terrified. Word that the magazine was about to explode spread through the city like wildfire. Soldiers were sent to knock on doors and get everyone out of the city. Mass hysteria followed. Everyone dropped what they were doing and ran. This left many trapped and injured victims to die in the fires.

Hordes of people stampeded through the streets. They headed towards the safety of open spaces. Before long, Citadel Hill, the Common, and Point Pleasant Park were filled with crowds of terrified souls. They waited nervously for the next blow to fall.

MacLennan had no idea that his actions had caused such a stir. He looked out to see his men scrambling to get through the hole in the fence. He dropped the extinguisher and began to follow. However, he couldn't get out. There were too many people trying to squeeze through the opening in the fence. MacLennan called out to a man outside the fence.

"What's all the panic about?" he asked.

"The roof of the magazine is on fire!" the man replied.

MacLennan paused and thought for a moment. There was no point running. If the magazine blew up, he'd be killed anyway. He took a deep breath. Then he climbed onto the roof to check the situation. The magazine was damaged all right. However, there was no evidence of fire. MacLennan still wasn't sure if the magazine was on fire or not. He decided to stick to his post anyway. He would do whatever he could to prevent a second explosion.

A few of MacLennan's recruits also stayed. The men went back to clearing out the magazine and hosing down the furnace room. They worked for several hours before the danger finally past.

While the threat of a second explosion hung over the city, Frances Coleman was unconscious. When she came to, she was jammed into an open wagon with several others. The wagon lurched along the rutted streets. Each rut they hit sent a jolt of pain through her.

Where were they going? She raised her head and looked around. To one side was a large, open field. She thought it must be the Common. A huge crowd swarmed the field. Frances wondered what was going on.

At last, the wagon stopped in front of Camp Hill Hospital. Frances was carried inside on a stretcher. The stretcher-bearers set her down among hundreds of others. Frances looked around the crowded room. It was a distressing sight. The foyer was overflowing with badly injured people. There were blackened, bloodied bodies everywhere. Sobs and moans filled the air.

After their mother had been taken to the hospital, the Coleman children weren't sure what to do. They couldn't go home. It was now a blazing ruin. The school was the same. They had no idea where their father was. Nor did they know if their mother would survive her injuries. Since Nita was the oldest, she took charge. She decided they should go to their Grandmother O'Toole's on Edward Street. It was in the South End of the city. Would it be a smouldering wreck as well? Nita feared it might be. However, she didn't mention her fears to her brother and sister.

After a few hours, the children finally reached their grandmother's house. They were relieved to see the house was still standing. Grandmother O'Toole was overjoyed to see them. She had been worried sick about her daughter and her grandchildren. She had heard rumours that Richmond had been wiped out in the blast. When Mrs. O'Toole hadn't heard from her daughter, she had feared the worst.

Meanwhile, the children's uncle, Chris Coleman, was out searching the city. He was looking for his brother Vincent and his family.

Mission of Mercy

When Jean Forrest arrived at Pier 2, she was shocked. The hospital was demolished. She was told to go to the Technical College on Spring Garden Road. There, a temporary Red Cross headquarters was being set up. It would also be a central medical supply depot. Jean wanted to gather whatever medical supplies she could find and get over to the devastated North End. She rushed to the college.

By the time Jean arrived, the college was in turmoil. Still, she managed to find bandages, dressings, and antiseptic. She loaded the supplies into the Red Cross car. Her plan was to drive to the North End and set up a first-aid station. However, Jean had never learned to drive. Before she could go, she had to find a chauffer. She asked a co-worker for help. He went out and found a man on the street who agreed to drive her to the North End.

The Red Cross worker and her driver only made it as far as North Street. There, they were stopped. Soldiers manning the barricade told them they weren't allowed into the area. Jean explained that she was a trained Red

Cross worker. She was there to help the victims. Still, the soldiers refused to let them in. Only firefighters and rescue workers were allowed to enter. Jean was frustrated. She asked the driver to take her back to the Red Cross headquarters.

Jean had just returned to the headquarters when an officer came in.

"There's a fire in the magazine at Wellington Barracks," he shouted. "Everyone get to the government field and lie flat!"

The other Red Cross workers dropped what they were doing. They headed for the Common. However, Jean was worried about her mother. She decided to go home instead.

Ground Zero

Dean Llwyd hurried through the smoke and raging fires to the heart of the ravaged area. He had never seen anything so awful. The entire area looked as though it had been bombarded. Little was left standing. He saw the remains of a factory, a wall or two of a house, and the odd telephone pole. Everything else was levelled. Fires raged all around. Mangled, blackened bodies were everywhere. Smoke stung Llwyd's eyes. The stench of burning flesh sickened him.

Streams of walking wounded passed by. Blood flowed from gashes on their heads and faces. Many groped along blindly. Some were missing arms or legs.

Others had limbs dangling from sockets. All were in a state of shock. Several people shouted at Llwyd to get out of the area. They told him there was going to be another explosion.

Llwyd kept going. In time, he came upon a group of soldiers. They were digging the wounded and dead out of the rubble. Llwyd joined them.

The officer in charge of the rescue party noticed Dean Llwyd's clerical collar. He asked what Llwyd thought they should do with the bodies. The minister suggested laying them out so they could be identified and picked up. Before long, the rescuers had more than 30 bodies lined up on the side of the road.

A Small Victory

From time to time, the men heard cries for help coming from the wreckage. Every now and then, they heard the shrill whinnying of horses in distress. At first, they thought the sounds came from spooked horses in the streets. However, the whinnying soon became more urgent. Finally, the officer in charge sent one of the soldiers off to look into it.

Before long, the soldier returned. He had found a stable full of terrified horses. They were trapped in the ruins. Fires were closing in all around them. The soldier had tried to free the horses himself, but he couldn't. He had come back for help. Hearing this, several of the men stopped what they were doing. They were about to rush off to rescue the horses. The officer ordered them back to work. He told them it was more important to save human lives than those of animals. A couple of soldiers were sent to help free the animals. The rest went back to work.

The thought of the trapped animals troubled everyone. They found it difficult to focus on the job at hand. After awhile, the whinnying stopped. Soon, the others returned with smiles on their faces. All the horses had been saved. This small victory raised everyone's spirits.

Rockhead Hospital

Josephine and Helen Crichton hadn't left the house that morning. They were sweeping up plaster and glass when a soldier came to the door. He told the sisters they must get out of the house. A second explosion might occur at any moment, he said. He told them to go to the Common or Point Pleasant Park. However, the girls were worried about their housebound friend. They hurried over to Queen Street. There, they found the elderly woman sitting in the middle of the street. She was an odd sight. She was all bundled up in blankets. Only her eyes could be seen, surrounded by soot-blackened skin. She looked so strange that she spooked every horse that came down the street.

Once the danger of another explosion passed, the girls took their friend inside and got her settled. Then they headed over to check on their 86-year-old aunt.

She lived on North Street. Josephine and Helen arrived to find their aunt sitting outside. Her house was still standing, but it was a shambles. Their aunt had a few minor cuts and bruises. Aside from that she was fine. The girls wanted to help her get the house back in order. She wouldn't hear of it. She insisted there were others in greater need.

"Don't stay here. We don't need you," she said. "We have our arms and legs. Go North! Go North!"

Josephine and Helen decided to go to Rockhead Hospital. On their way, they stopped at Logan's Drug Store. They wanted to pick up some medical supplies. The store was deserted. Its large, plate glass window was shattered. Inside, a thick crust of glass and plaster covered the floor. The shelves were knocked over. The merchandise was buried in the debris. The only useful items they found were one roll of adhesive tape and a small bottle of antiseptic. The girls felt guilty for taking the items without paying for them. However, they needed the supplies and there was no clerk on hand. What else could they do?

The sights on the streets were ghastly. Josephine and Helen kept going. Along the way, they noticed a huge fire in the distance. They detoured to get a look at the blaze at the Cotton Factory. Then they carried on.

Rockhead Hospital sat on a bluff next to Rockhead Prison. It overlooked the Bedford Basin and the Narrows. It had taken the full brunt of the blast. The reinforced concrete walls were still standing. However, the building was a wreck. The doors and windows were splintered and smashed. The roof had partially collapsed, and the pipes had burst.

There were 80 patients in the hospital at the time. They were all wounded soldiers returned from France. Many had given up their beds to people worse off than themselves. Those who were able carried out nursing and orderly duties.

All of the beds from the upper floors had been moved down to the lower floors. There was barely enough room to squeeze between the rows. Rockhead was like every other hospital in the city that day. It was crammed with wounded and dying victims of the explosion. There were three or four children to a bed. Many victims lay on mattresses on the floor. In one office, Josephine found a dozen wounded children lying on the floor.

There were only two doctors in the hospital that day. The Crichton sisters reported to the doctor in charge. He told them to bathe and dress the minor wounds but to leave the bad ones alone. These were better "with the blood congealed," he said.

It was terribly cold in the roofless, windowless building. To stay warm, the girls kept their coats and hats on. Several centimetres of water lay on the floor in places. Neither of the girls was wearing boots. To keep their shoes dry, they had to walk on their heels through the flooded areas.

Josephine and Helen worked from the time they arrived until the time they left the next afternoon. They dressed wounds and assisted the doctors. They tried to keep the patients warm by bringing them hot cups of tea. They also passed out warm bricks to heat the beds. The sisters were surprised at how selfless their patients were. Everyone seemed more concerned about the welfare of others than about themselves.

Chapter 8
Exodus

By 11 a.m. some order had been restored on the *Niobe*. Fred Longland was told to take a platoon out to search the streets and morgues for dead sailors. The navy uniforms had bell-bottomed trousers. Longland and his crew were told to watch for the bell-bottoms. Whenever they saw a pair, they were to dig out the body and lay it aside for pick up.

It was a gruesome task. The carnage in the streets was terrible. The morgue was just as bad. There, soldiers carried in load after load of mutilated bodies. The bodies were cleaned. Then they were laid out to be identified. After hours of searching, Longland returned to the *Niobe* for a break.

Meanwhile, Evelyn Fox left the academy with her schoolmates, Patsy and Rose. The three girls headed north. They began to realize their school wasn't the only building affected by the blast. All along Brunswick Street, windows had been smashed out. Doors were blown off their hinges. The girls met several people along the way. They all seemed to be in a strange, "trance-like state."

The girls finally arrived at Evelyn's father's school. Alexandra School was farther north than the Academy. It had suffered far more damage. The chaos inside took Evelyn by surprise. "Shreds of green blinds flapped at paneless windows, or were strewn across the floor where broken desks lay upon their sides, and slashed books and papers (many impaled upon long glass stilettos) mingled with inches-deep plaster and glass."

When Evelyn arrived, her father was bandaging a gash on a boy's hand. Her father's face was pinched and pale. When he caught sight of her, the worried frown vanished.

"Douglas is all right," he said. "He stopped here on his way back to barracks to report for special duty."

Douglas was Evelyn's older brother. He was a soldier stationed at the Brunswick Street Barracks. Until then, it had not occurred to Evelyn to be concerned about her family. Mr. Fox saw the bewildered look on his daughter's face. He realized she had no idea of exactly what had happened.

"A munitions ship blew up in the Narrows," he explained.

This explained things a bit. However, Evelyn still

had not grasped the extent of the disaster.

Before she left, Evelyn promised her father she would wait for him at the train station. On their way out, the girls ran into Hazel. She was another friend from Bedford. The four girls left the school together. They kept heading north. The farther north they went, the worse the damage was. The houses were destroyed. Most only had a wall or two left standing.

The street corner by the train station was usually bustling. Evelyn noticed it was all but deserted that afternoon. The stillness seemed strange. A few horse-drawn carts loaded with refugees passed by. Other carts carried casualties to the hospital. Suddenly, the quiet was shattered. Four soldiers came running down the street.

"Fire! Wellington Barracks Magazine is on fire! Move south. Into the open! Everybody south!" they shouted.

Evelyn's three friends started to run. Evelyn stayed where she was. When the girls realized Evelyn wasn't following them, they turned back. Evelyn was torn. Should she obey her father's order to wait for him at the train station? Or should she follow the soldiers' command to move south? She decided to go with her friends.

Before long, the girls were sitting on the eastern slope of Citadel Hill. They were surrounded by hundreds of others. The crowd was silent. They crouched on the grass and stared northwards. Most people were not dressed for the weather. Many wore nothing but a nightgown or pyjamas. Some had bare feet or wore only slippers. Evelyn was glad she had managed to get her coat before leaving the school. It was a bright, mild day for December. It was still far too cold to be outside without a coat.

Pillars of black smoke hovered over the North End of the city. The fear of another explosion grew among the jittery crowd. They had already suffered so much that day. The Citadel seemed too close to the danger for them. Many decided to move farther west, "away from the harbour's munitions ships and possible enemies, away from the fort's magazines." Evelyn became caught up in the adventure of it all. She forgot about meeting her father by the train station. Instead, she and her friends fell in with the mass of people leaving the city.

The victims were like the refugees of a war-torn nation. They fled with whatever was left of their belongings. A line of horse-drawn carts, wagons, and automobiles moved across the city and out St. Margaret's Bay Road. Every vehicle was loaded with shell-shocked survivors in search of safety.

Evelyn and her friends walked many kilometres. At last, they could go no farther. They stopped at a field. There, clusters of people were crowded around small fires. A tall, thin soldier invited the girls to share his fire. He told them his name was Laurence. He had been wounded overseas and sent home to recover. After the explosion, the soldier had given up his bed in Camp Hill Hospital. There were others who needed it more than him, he said. The girls asked him where he would sleep that night. Laurence told them not to worry. He was used to sleeping outdoors in his greatcoat. This reminded Evelyn of her older brother, Ashford. He was currently serving in France. She thought of her brother sleeping out on the cold, wet ground with nothing but his greatcoat to keep him warm. Suddenly, the war seemed very real and very close to home.

The Number 10 Train
The Number 10 Train had been late that morning. As it crept towards Rockingham, Andrew Cobb glanced out at Bedford Basin. Dozens of ships were anchored in the basin. It looked like another convoy was preparing to set sail. The sight of the vessels cast a shadow over the perfect morning. After three long years, it seemed like the war was going to drag on forever.

All of a sudden, a terrible blast jolted the train. It felt as though it had been smacked by a giant hand. The cars tipped up at a shaky angle. Then they dropped back to the tracks with a crash. The windows lining the car shattered. Shrieks filled the air. Then everything grew still. What could have caused such a tremendous blast? Several minutes passed. Then the train began to creep towards the city.

Africville was the small African-Canadian community on the northern tip of the peninsula. The passengers were relieved to see that it looked undamaged. However, just outside of Richmond, the tracks became impassable. The train came to a full stop.

Suddenly, hundreds of wounded and desperate people appeared. They swarmed the train begging for help. They looked frightful. Most were covered with a black, oily-looking substance. In addition to being filthy, the victims' clothes were ragged and blood-soaked. Several people carried their wounded in bloodied sheets. Others stumbled along with towels or pillows pressed against wounds to stop the bleeding. Something had to be done to help the victims. It seemed the only option was to take them aboard.

The conductor decided to dump the baggage and mail bags. He wanted to make room for as many of the wounded as possible. The passengers got to work at once. The men began unloading the baggage. Then they lifted the injured onto the train. The women raided the dining car and sleeping compartments for table linens and bedding. They tore the linens into strips for bandages. Everyone tried to make the victims comfortable.

Many of the wounded needed medical help. However, there was no doctor onboard. Andrew Cobb volunteered to go in search of one. Cobb headed off into the devastated area. He soon realized his search was hopeless, and he turned back.

By the time Andrew Cobb returned to the train, a military doctor had come aboard. The doctor was busy tending to the wounded. Things seemed to be under control on the train. Cobb and six others decided to start searching through the ruins for victims. Before long, they came across four people in need of help. A man and his wife, and another woman and her small son were trapped beneath a house.

The rescuers could hear the victims shrieking and sobbing beneath the rubble. They shouted out directions to the men. The rescuers worked feverishly to find them. The job was almost impossible. Large sections of roof and walls were too heavy for the men to lift. They had to be torn apart before they could be removed. The trouble was, the rescuers had only their bare hands to work with. To make matters worse, the house next door was on fire. Four children were trapped inside the burning house. The children's parents and several others were working to rescue them. It was clear from the strength of the fire and the children's cries, that they were being burned alive. The children's tortured cries for help were heart-wrenching.

After several gruelling hours, Cobb and the others finally managed to free the victims. The man wasn't hurt, but his wife was badly injured. Her face was deeply slashed and one eye had been gouged out. The other woman and her son had only minor cuts and bruises. All four were in shock, but they were grateful to be alive.

Once the family was freed, Andrew Cobb was drained. He left the others and set out for his office on Barrington Street. The sun was still shining brightly.

However, a thick layer of smoke shrouded the entire North End of the city. Tangles of downed wires, poles, and debris made walking difficult. Bodies were scattered everywhere. Cobb felt sick at heart. Would the city ever recover from such a disaster?

Meanwhile, the Number 10 Train's conductor was not sure what to do next. He had a trainload of casualties. However, he couldn't get into the city to get them to hospital. He wasn't able to contact his superiors for instructions. He decided to turn back to Rockingham. There, he might be able to make contact.

Once in Rockingham, the conductor finally got through to head office. It was decided he should take the train to Truro. This was a small town about an hour away. There, the patients would receive medical care.

Chapter 9
Casualties and Compassion

Charles Duggan rushed down the gangplank the minute the ferry docked. He was still soaking wet from being plunged into the harbour. Outside, he quickly grew numb with cold. He stopped in at McCartney's Billiard Hall to warm up. Then he kept going northwards. When he reached North Street, soldiers had roped off the area. He begged them to let him in. He explained that his family was in the area. Still, they refused to let him enter. Charles decided to go to his sister's place on North Street. He hoped she would have some news of their family.

Charles was happy to find his sister unharmed. However, she had horrific news. The rest of the Duggan family had all been killed in the explosion. Charles' wife Rita and son Warren, his mother and father, his brother, and two other sisters were all dead. Charles was stunned by the news. He remembered the cries for help he had heard on the Dartmouth shore. Had some of those cries come from his family? He felt he would never get those sounds out of his head.

The Cotton Factory

Once again Jean Forrest prepared to go to the North End. This time, she found a returned soldier to drive her. Luckily, the soldier knew a way around the restricted area. They could drive up North Street and down Robie. This route took them out past the Cotton Factory.

The large factory employed around 300 people. It was now a "seething mass of flames." Heavy machinery had crashed through the ceilings from the upper floors. Many workers had been crushed to death. Others were pinned beneath machinery, beams, and concrete. Unable to free themselves, they burned to death in the fire. Hundreds of workers in other factories shared the same tragic fate that day.

In the fields beyond the factory, Jean found a crowd of people. Many were seriously injured and needed medical attention. Jean and the soldier loaded several victims into the car and headed for the hospital. It was slow going. The streets were clogged with wagons, cars, and trucks. All were taking patients to the hospitals. Downed electrical wires, glass, and debris slowed traffic to a crawl.

Jean and the soldier dropped off the first load of patients. Then they headed back for another. After a few trips, the car's tires began to blow out. One by one, the tires went flat. Then, they fell off. Jean and her driver didn't let that stop them. They wanted to save as many lives as possible. Finally, they were driving on nothing but the rims.

A little girl was in the last load of patients they delivered to the hospital. There was no room for the girl's mother in the car. However, she didn't want to let her daughter go without her. She had heard of several mothers being separated from their children that day. She was terrified of losing her daughter. Jean knew there was no time to waste. The girl had to get to the hospital. She promised to come back and tell the mother which hospital her daughter was in. Jean's promise comforted the woman. She finally agreed to let her daughter go.

The Relief Train
By 11:30 a.m., word of the disaster hadn't reached the town of Kentville in the Annapolis Valley. Dr. Willis Moore was getting ready to make a house call. Just before he left his office, an urgent message arrived. There had been a disaster in Halifax. A special relief train carrying doctors, nurses, and supplies was preparing to leave for the city. Dr. Moore was asked to join them. The doctor quickly gathered all the instruments and supplies he could carry. He closed his office and

rushed down to the station. By the time he arrived, a number of doctors and nurses were already boarding the train.

At Windsor Junction, they stopped to take on more medical supplies. There, they met the night express from Saint John. It was known as the Number 10 Train. The night express had just come from Halifax. It was a shocking sight. The train looked as though it had just returned from the front lines of battle. Its windows were all shattered. The battered cars were packed with casualties.

Major Avery DeWitt was the military doctor aboard the Number 10. He had come in from Camp Aldershot for a meeting that morning. Luckily, he had brought his medical bag along. There were more than 200 critically wounded men, women, and children on the train. This was far more than one doctor could manage. Meeting the trainload of doctors and nurses at Windsor Junction was a godsend to those aboard the Number 10. A doctor and nurse from the train bound for Halifax joined the train going to Truro. Both trains carried on their separate ways. During the journey to Truro, Major DeWitt worked at one end of the train. The other doctor and nurse were stationed at the other end. The conditions were cramped. Yet, DeWitt performed two successful eye operations along the way. Three children died before they reached their destination. However, many lives were saved aboard the rolling hospital.

The relief train carrying Dr. Moore arrived at the outskirts of the city about 3 p.m. The crumpled tracks and mounds of debris stopped them from going any farther. The doctors and nurses got off the train and began walking. The horrific sights along the way sickened Dr. Moore. Everywhere he looked, there were "rows of blackened and often half-naked and twisted bodies." The extent of the ruins was beyond belief, especially along the waterfront. It was a depressing scene. The doctors and nurses hurried through the area. They were anxious to begin helping the victims.

Camp Hill Hospital

Finally, they arrived at Camp Hill Hospital. In some ways, the sights there were worse than those in the streets. Camp Hill was a brand-new facility. It had been built for wounded soldiers returning from overseas. After the explosion, the two-storey building was a shambles. Blankets, tar paper, and boards covered the smashed windows. Out front, a parade of cars, trucks, wheelbarrows, and horses and wagons came and went. They delivered load after load of wounded and dying.

Inside, the dark corridors and wards were crowded with victims. The space was designed to hold fewer than 250 people. That day, 1,400 men, women, and children were packed inside. Every square metre of space was used. Mattresses lined the corridors. Casualties were crammed into offices. Even storage rooms were jammed with patients. According to one witness, "Men, women, and children were literally packed into the wards like sardines in a box." Dr. Moore had never seen so many people in such desperate need.

Dr. Moore was shown to a makeshift operating room. There, he began trying to mend the battered and broken bodies. One by one, they were carried into the operating room. Faces were sliced open. Limbs were ripped off. Eyeballs were studded with glass. The lighting was very bad. It was difficult for the doctor to see what he was doing. To make matters worse, he didn't have the proper equipment and supplies. Nor was there enough antiseptic or anaesthetic to go around. In many cases, operations were performed without either. The doctors soon ran out of surgical thread. However, this didn't stop them. They began using ordinary cotton thread to stitch up the wounds.

The doctors worked non-stop for hours. After a while, the strain began to take its toll. At one point, a volunteer accidentally knocked over a tray of surgical instruments. Dr. Moore flew at her in a rage. Then he felt bad. He apologized right away. He helped her pick up the instruments, and he got back to work.

The greatest numbers of injuries were caused by flying glass. Hundreds of people had crowded around windows to get a look at the burning ship. Most were blinded when the windows shattered. Others were horribly disfigured by the flying glass. Noses, lips, and cheeks were gashed or cut completely off. One woman's face was sliced almost entirely off. She died before doctors could get to her. Many others with similar wounds survived.

At one point, Dr. Moore was asked to look at an urgent case. Two female victims had just arrived. They lay side by side on a bloody mattress. One of the women was already dead. Her body was half-naked. It did not have a mark on it. The other was horribly mutilated. One eye was gone. The other eye was badly injured. Her face was badly slashed. She would be "blinded and disfigured for life." Yet she had a strong pulse. She was expected to live.

The Shelters

While doctors and nurses fought to save lives, city officials struggled to restore order. At 3 p.m., Deputy Mayor Colwell and the lieutenant governor met with other members of City Council. They organized committees to deal with the disaster. Six committees were set up. They included transportation, distribution of food and clothing, disposal of the dead, finance, and shelter for the homeless.

Housing was critical. Before the disaster, the city had been short of housing. Now, thousands more were on the streets. The committee decided that any undamaged public buildings would be used as shelters. These included the theatre, the Academy of Music, and parish halls. The Salvation Army and the Knights of Columbus also offered space for shelters.

Blankets, cots, and bedding were rounded up. Partitions were quickly put up. Washroom facilities were created. By early evening, many of the shelters opened their doors. People began pouring in. They were grateful to have a place to sleep that night. Dozens of private homes also took in as many refugees as they could hold. Still, there wasn't enough space to house everyone. Many people were forced to sleep in the streets. They huddled in doorways, abandoned buildings, and alleys. Many slept wherever they could find a place to curl up.

Dean Llwyd had worked for several hours in the ruins. He needed a break. He decided to go to City Hall to arrange for the disposal of the bodies. At City Hall, he met with the deputy mayor and the committee in charge of looking after the dead. The committee's first task was to find a place to put the bodies. The Chebucto Road School was undamaged. It was just outside the devastated area. The group decided to use the school as a mortuary.

Afterwards, Llwyd went home to clean up. Then he headed over to Camp Hill Hospital. He was very tired, but he felt it was his duty to comfort the victims. The scene at the hospital was "heartrending." Several victims were badly mangled. Many were bathed in blood. Others were soaked from the tidal wave or from being plunged into the harbour. With the windows smashed and the doors constantly opening, the hospital was very cold. Patients in wet clothing suffered terribly. Many died of exposure.

In the turmoil following the explosion, hundreds of parents and children had become separated. That afternoon, Llwyd was troubled by the sight of parents searching the wards for missing children. The cries of badly wounded children for absent parents were even more troubling. He knew that the sights he saw that afternoon would haunt him forever.

In the midst of the horror and misery, Dean Llwyd also witnessed goodness. The outpouring of generosity and goodwill warmed his heart. Volunteers and nurses worked tirelessly. They dressed wounds and tried to ease the patients' suffering. He was awed by their skill and caring. Many women had lost their own homes and family members that day. However, they didn't think twice about rushing to the aid of others. Hospital volunteers worked around the clock. No one complained.

That day, the explosion was the only thing people talked about. How had it happened? Who was responsible? Some of the injured had been on ships in the harbour at the time. They told Llwyd their stories. Most claimed the French ship was at fault. One officer described what he had seen. "It was as though the French ship burst asunder," the man said, "and showed a raging furnace within."

The Abandoned Baby

Evelyn Fox and her friends stayed in the field off St. Margaret's Bay Road until late in the afternoon. While they were there, a young woman with a baby came along. The woman's dress was torn and dirty. Her face was smeared with soot. She looked very tired. The girls offered to hold the baby while the woman rested by the fire. They thought the young woman was the baby's mother. Hazel asked its name.

"I haven't any idea," the woman replied. She explained how she got the baby. Her house had collapsed in the explosion. Luckily, she managed to escape before it burned down. Outside, there was total chaos. "All around people were running or trapped and screaming in the fires," she said. "I ran. Someone put this baby in my arms. I kept running."

The story astonished the girls. They noticed the baby wasn't wearing any hat or coat. Its gown was bloodstained. Who were its parents? Were they searching through smoking rubble for their child? Or had they died in the explosion? The girls worried about what would happen to the infant.

The young woman rested for a few minutes. Then she rose to leave. Hazel went to hand the baby over to her. The woman backed away.

"I haven't anyone to turn to and nowhere to go," she said. "The baby will be better off with you girls."

Then she turned and tramped across the field

towards the road.

The baby was hungry and needed changing. It howled constantly. The girls took turns trying to soothe it. Evelyn held it close to her body to keep it warm. She wished there was something she could do to comfort the child.

After a time, a young woman came along. She was driving a cart. On the back of the cart were several cold and dirty children. The woman jumped down. She shuffled over to the fire. The girls noticed that the woman was oddly dressed. She wore a pair of men's rubber boots. A man's overcoat hung from her narrow shoulders. Beneath the coat was a grimy looking dress.

"I heard a baby crying," she said.

The girls showed her the baby. They explained how they had got it. "The baby won't stop crying," they wailed.

"I'd better take it," said the woman. "I have relatives 10 miles farther on. If I can get that far, they'll have milk."

The girls were relieved to hand over the baby. The woman gently tucked it beneath her overcoat. She climbed back onto the cart. Then she gave the reins a snap and plodded away.

After the woman left, Evelyn felt exhausted. The effort of trying to comfort the baby had worn her out. She suddenly realized she was "cold, hungry and miles from home." She wondered where her father was. Was he worried about her?

Meanwhile, Captain Aimé Le Medec and his crew were wandering around outside Dartmouth. The men were lost and dazed. One crew member was badly wounded. They took turns carrying him as they searched for a doctor.

Late in the afternoon, the captain and crew of the *Mont Blanc* came upon a rescue party. The rescue workers were from the *Highflyer*. The French captain identified himself and asked for help finding a doctor. The officer in charge decided that the French crew should be taken back to the *Highflyer*. They would be kept aboard the British cruiser until an investigation could be held.

The Promise

By 4 p.m., the Red Cross car had broken down. Jean Forrest and her driver left it by the side of the road. They looked around for another car. Every vehicle in the city was being used to ferry victims to hospitals. Jean worried about keeping the promise she had made earlier. The mother of the girl they'd taken to the hospital would be anxious about her daughter. She was determined to find a way to get word to the woman.

Try as she might, Jean couldn't find a car or a ride. Finally, she decided to walk back to the fields beyond the Cotton Factory. She arrived at dusk. She found the girl's mother huddled by a fire. Jean told her that her daughter was at Camp Hill Hospital. She was being looked after. When she heard the news, the woman's eyes shone with gratitude.

Sailors were passing out cake and bread to the hungry crowd in the field. However, there was nothing for them to drink. Jean decided to look for some milk or juice to go with the bread. She hadn't noticed any stores along Robie Street, the route she and the soldier had been driving along most of the day. She decided to look for a place on Gottingen Street. She noticed all the stores were burned or boarded up. Jean was stunned. The destruction in this area was terrible. All day, she had been on the outskirts of the devastated area. She had thought that was as bad as it got. Now she realized that things were much worse than she had imagined.

The Mysterious Patient

After his stint in the North End, Fred Longland made his way back to the *Niobe.* Just as he sat down, a commander came looking for him. Someone at the Victoria General Hospital had asked for him, the commander said. Longland couldn't imagine who it could be. He had just arrived back in town. He didn't know many people here. Still, he hurried over to the hospital.

At the Victoria General, Fred was shown to the bedside of a man. He was unconscious. Fred looked closely at the patient. The man was "pitted all over with what looked like bits of cinder. He was a nasty yellow colour." Fred didn't recognize him. The staff told him the only thing the patient had said since arriving was "Fred Longland." Fred was puzzled. He couldn't figure out who the mysterious man might be. He asked the staff to contact him if the patient's condition changed. Then he returned to the *Niobe*.

Three weeks later, the patient came out of his coma. Once again the hospital contacted Longland. He went to see the man. This time, the patient was sitting up. He looked much better. It turned out the stranger had been friends with Fred when they were children. The man had remembered hearing that Fred Longland was serving in Halifax. This fact stuck with him even though he was in a coma. The whole time he was unconscious, Fred's was the only name he spoke.

The Journey Home

As the day wore on, Evelyn Fox lost her sense of adventure. She longed for the safety and comfort of home. Evelyn and her friends weren't sure if it was safe to go back to the city. By then, the danger of a second explosion had passed. People were now allowed to return home. However, the news hadn't reached those in the outlying areas. The girls decided to take the chance anyway. They invited Laurence to come home with them. At first, Laurence refused. He said that he would be fine sleeping outside in his greatcoat. The girls wouldn't hear of it. Finally, he gave in. The group set out along the railway tracks heading for Fairview.

Laurence trailed along after them.

Rockingham was six kilometres past the devastated North End. When they reached Rockingham, it was growing dark. An idling train sat on the tracks. It was the most welcome sight Evelyn had seen all day. She and her friends climbed aboard.

The cars were crowded with wounded and homeless people from the city. The city hospitals and shelters were all overflowing. Any victims who were able to make the trip were being sent elsewhere. This train was on its way to Truro and points beyond. There, the victims would be given shelter and medical treatment. Evelyn noticed that everyone onboard was strangely silent. Most people seemed to be in a deep state of shock.

The journey home was tense. The sisters had invited Laurence to stay at their place. Now they started to worry about the invitation. How would their parents react to them dragging home a soldier they had just met? Finally, Evelyn settled the matter.

"I have a brother in France," she said. "If our house is still standing, there'll be room in it for a returned soldier."

By the time they arrived in Bedford, it was pitch black outside. The girls said their goodbyes at the station and went their separate ways. Evelyn stumbled through the darkness towards home. Laurence limped along behind her. She had not spent much time that day worrying about her family. Now, she was filled with guilt and worry. Would the house still be standing? Would her father be out searching the city for her? Would her mother, brothers, and sister be all right?

They finally arrived home. Evelyn was almost afraid to go inside. The house was completely dark. It was impossible to tell if anyone was home. She took a deep breath and opened the door. A warm glow of lamplight was coming from the kitchen. She stepped in to find her whole family sitting around the table waiting for her.

Evelyn introduced Laurence. She explained that he had given up his bed at Camp Hill Hospital. He had nowhere to sleep that night. Mr. Fox warmly shook the soldier's hand. He took Laurence's greatcoat from him. Then he pulled another chair up to the table.

The Morgue

At 6 p.m., the makeshift morgue in the basement of the Chebucto Road School opened its doors. Those looking for missing family members could come in. By that time, a long line of desperate people were waiting outside. Chris Coleman was one of them. He had searched for his brother Vincent everywhere that day. He had scoured every hospital and shelter in the city. Earlier, he had found his sister-in-law, Frances, in Camp Hill Hospital. Chris had promised her he would return with word of Vincent as soon as he could. Now, he waited in line with hundreds of others. They had come to the morgue as a last resort. Everyone hoped they wouldn't find what they were looking for inside. Finally, Chris's turn came to enter the morgue. He followed the soldier down into the cold, dimly lit basement. It was lined with row upon row of white-sheeted mounds.

Chapter 10
No End in Sight

Dr. Moore had been stitching up wounds for hours. He was beyond exhaustion. He knew he had to take a break. Then he would continue into the night. The doctor was worried about his relatives in Dartmouth. He'd heard it had also been hard hit by the explosion. The telephones weren't working. There was only one way Moore could contact his relatives. He had to go there in person.

A co-worker also had relatives across the harbour. He offered to go with Moore. No cars or taxis were available so the two men set out on foot. The streets were hazardous. There was no electricity or gas. Even if there had been, the streets would still be dark. Due to the war, a blackout order was in effect. That meant streetlights were not turned on at night. Windows were covered so no light would shine out. This left the city cloaked in darkness. The men could barely see two steps ahead in the gloom. Still, they hurried through the darkness to the ferry terminal.

The ferry churned across the dark harbour. Dr. Moore and his co-worker stood on deck. They stared back at the ravaged city. The fires still raged in the North End. The city looked strange in the firelight's reddish-orange glow.

Dr. Moore was relieved when he finally arrived at his relatives' home. They had escaped with only minor injuries and property damage. After a short visit, he headed back across the harbour. Before he returned to the hospital, he was to check on some victims in the North End. They had not been taken to the hospital. However, they needed medical attention.

For the second time that day, the elderly doctor made his way through the ruins. He got to the battered house just as it began to snow. The victims were huddled together in the dimly lit room. Carpets and boards were nailed up over the windows and doors. Still, the cold and snow swirled in through cracks and crevices.

Meanwhile, the Brannen family struggled to cope with the tragic events of the day. Captain Horatio Brannen's wife Susie had been told of his death. The news was devastating. What's more, she wasn't sure if her son Walter was dead or alive. It was not until that evening that she got word he was alive.

When he finally arrived home, Walter was a dreadful sight. His face was bruised and bandaged. Most of his clothes had been ripped off in the explosion. A red tablecloth was draped over his shoulders to keep him from freezing. Walter was in a deep state of shock. It was a miracle that he and William Knickerson had survived the explosion. Everyone around them had died. Yet, their wounds were not too serious. These physical wounds would heal in time. The emotional scars would be with them forever.

By nightfall, Lieutenant Charles MacLennan and his men were still at the magazine at Wellington Barracks. They prepared to stay on duty through the night. MacLennan was tired, hungry, and cold. Still, he was determined to remain at his post. He and his men hadn't eaten a thing since breakfast. MacLennan decided to go out in search of rations. Not far from the barracks, he discovered a bread cart. It had overturned in the explosion. The bread had spilled out onto the street. MacLennan grabbed as many loaves as he could carry. He rushed back to the magazine to feed his hungry men.

Until that day, the weather had been unusually mild. There had been very little snow. That night, the temperature dropped. A fierce blizzard blew in. MacLennan and his men found some poles and a few animal hides in the magazine. With these, they made a crude shelter. Throughout the night, the exhausted men huddled beneath the hides trying to stay warm.

Across town, Jean Forrest was returning to the Technical College. Her legs and feet ached. She had been crisscrossing the city all day. She had taken dozens of people to the hospital. In addition, she had comforted and treated the wounds of many more. However, she wasn't finished her errands of mercy. There were still so many people who needed help. How could she worry about herself when thousands were in such desperate need?

At the Red Cross headquarters, dozens of volunteers were tearing sheets into strips. The strips were rolled into bandages. Jean pitched in to help. Just then, a supervisor came along and asked her to carry supplies around to the hospitals.

Jean loaded up as many supplies as she could carry. Then she set out once again. The cobblestone streets were covered with a slippery layer of snow. Jean slipped and stumbled several times as she hurried along. Finally, she arrived at the Victoria General Hospital.

There were several makeshift hospitals and dressing stations opened all over the city by then. Still, the Victoria General was overflowing. People were forced to wait outside. Victims shivered with cold as they waited for care. It was heart-wrenching to see them. Jean wished she could do something to stop their suffering. However, there were still many hospitals left to visit that night.

At Camp Hill Hospital, the sights and sounds in the ward were horrific. Frances Coleman closed her eyes. She tried to shut it all out. Her brother-in-law, Chris Coleman, had been in earlier. He had brought heartbreaking news.

Chris had searched all day for his brother. He had finally found Vincent's remains at the morgue. Vincent Coleman had died at his post. He had been tapping out a warning to incoming trains to stay clear. The dispatcher had sacrificed his own life to try to save hundreds of others. He had died a hero.

Frances was just 40 years old. She had already lost her father and a son. Now she had lost her husband as well. After Chris left, she tried to sleep. Thoughts of Vincent, her children, and the tragic events of the day kept running through her mind. It seemed the pain and sorrow of this day would never end.

12 a.m. December 7, 1917

The devastated city lay cloaked in blackness. Despite the cold and dark, rescue workers were still combing the ruins for victims. Meanwhile, the presses at the *Morning Chronicle* were churning out the next day's paper. The headline shouted: "HALIFAX IN RUINS." And below that:

> *Collision which occurred at 9:05 yesterday morning has laid the Northern End of the city in ruins. Mont Blanc a French munitions*

boat collides in the harbour with a Belgian relief ship and blows up. — Dead number hundreds and casualties are known to be in the thousands. — Every available place in the city being utilized as emergency morgues and hospitals — No cause yet found for the collision — Crowds of frenzied people rush through streets fleeing from what was first thought to be a German raid — Streets littered with dead — Practically two square miles of territory a burning ruin.

Outside, the worst blizzard to hit Halifax in years was gathering force. It made search and rescue almost impossible. The fires continued to rage in the North End. Snow blew in blinding swirls around Citadel Hill. It drifted in mounds around the tent city on the Common. In the harbour, gale-force winds lashed battered ships. Crews worked frantically to secure the unmoored vessels. Those whose houses were still standing tried to keep warm by the fire. Snow gusted in around hastily boarded up windows and doors. Few would sleep that night.

Epilogue

The Halifax Explosion happened on December 6, 1917. It was the worst explosion caused by humans before Hiroshima. More than 130 hectares of the city were laid waste. The exact number of deaths will never be known. It is estimated that 2,000 or more lives were lost. In addition, 9,000 people were injured. Hundreds were permanently blinded. Of those who did survive, 20,000 found themselves homeless and poverty-stricken. They lost everything they owned. Many also lost one or more family members that day. The survivors faced a grim winter as they tried to rebuild their shattered lives.

For weeks after the explosion, the local newspapers ran columns listing the dead, the missing, and those in hospitals. These lists were many pages long. Day after day, notices appeared describing children that had been found. Others were seeking missing persons. Eight days after the blast, there were still 350 unidentified bodies in the morgue. Soldiers were still digging bodies from the ruins. Family members were still searching for missing loved ones. Dozens of infants and young children were orphaned. Many children were separated from their parents. Some never were reunited.

Windows all across the city shattered in the blast. The flying glass blinded hundreds of people. After the explosion, doctors performed hundreds of operations to remove badly injured eyes. At the Victoria General Hospital alone, 60 operations of this kind were done in a single day.

The explosion also left many survivors scarred for life. Faces were marred by cuts, burns, and pits caused by flying shrapnel. Years later, survivors were still picking shards of glass from beneath their skin. In time, the physical scars healed. The emotional scars took much longer. Many victims had complete nervous and mental breakdowns. They could not come to terms with the horror and trauma they had experienced that day. Many committed suicide. Others lived in constant fear of another explosion. Loud noises or fire often made survivors panic.

Word of the explosion quickly spread. Before long, aid began pouring in from all over the world. The American response was very generous. Relief trains from Boston and New York brought food, medical supplies, and equipment. Many more relief trains followed.

A Massachusetts–Halifax Relief Committee was set up. The people of that state gave generously to their northern neighbours. They sent shiploads of glass, lumber, building supplies, and new trucks to Halifax. Massachusetts also sent loads of clothing, blankets, and food. Trade workers came to help rebuild the city. Dozens of carpenters, engineers, construction workers, glaziers, and plumbers offered their skills. A plea for doctors and nurses brought hundreds from all over the East Coast.

Sir John Eaton was president of the Timothy Eaton Company in Toronto. Eaton donated millions of dollars worth of medical supplies and equipment, clothing, building materials, and household goods. Eaton delivered these goods in person. He even oversaw their distribution.

It wasn't only the rich and powerful who gave to the relief effort. People from all across Canada donated whatever they could. Schoolchildren emptied their piggy banks for the cause. Girl Guides and Boy Scouts collected funds for the children of Halifax. All this generosity helped the city to recover. However, it would be many years before the damage was repaired and life returned to normal.

Further Reading

Bird, Michael J. *The Town that Died: The True Story of the Greatest Man-Made Explosion Before Hiroshima.* Toronto: McGraw-Hill Ryerson Ltd., 1962.

Kitz, Janet F. *Shattered City: The Halifax Explosion and the Road to Recovery.* Halifax: Nimbus Publishing, 1989.

MacLennan, Hugh. *Barometer Rising.* Toronto: McCelelland & Stewart Inc., 1989.

MacMechan, Archibald. "The Halifax Disaster" in *The Halifax Explosion: December 6, 1917.* Toronto: McGraw-Hill Ryerson Ltd., 1978.

Mahar, James and Rownea Mahar. *Too Many To Mourn: One Family's Tragedy in the Halifax Explosion.* Halifax: Nimbus, 1998.

Richardson, Evelyn M. "The Halifax Explosion — 1917." *The Nova Scotia Historical Quarterly* Vol. 7 No. 4., 1977.

Acknowledgements

I am indebted to many people for their generous assistance in the creation of this book. Heartfelt thanks to Janette Snooks and Anne Finlayson for graciously sharing memories and information about their parents and grandparents, Vincent and Frances Coleman; Jim Simpson for the insightful tour of the explosion sites; Dan Conlin, Curator of Maritime History at the Maritime Museum of the Atlantic, for his helpful advice and assistance; the staff at the Provincial Archives of Nova Scotia; Alan Ruffman for his advice and suggestions; Douglas Shand for the biographical material on Evelyn Richardson; and Brian Cuthbertson, archivist at All Saints Cathedral, for the information on Dean Llwyd.

Thanks also to Kara Turner at Altitude Publishing for giving me the opportunity to tell this amazing story. Finally, this book would not have been possible without the support and encouragement of my husband, Doug, and my family.

About the Author

Joyce Glasner is also the author of *Christmas in Atlantic Canada: Heartwarming Legends, Tales, and Traditions;* and *Pirates and Privateers: Swashbuckling Stories from the East Coast.* She lives in Halifax, Nova Scotia.

Photo Credits

National Archive of Canada: cover, pages 38-39
Nova Scotia Archives: page 4, 33